Eva O'Connor

Maz and Bricks

Bloomsbury Methuen Drama
An imprint of Bloomsbury Publishing Plc

B L O O M S B U R Y
LONDON · OXFORD · NEW YORK · NEW DELHI · SYDNEY

Bloomsbury Methuen Drama

An imprint of Bloomsbury Publishing Plc

Imprint previously known as Methuen Drama

50 Bedford Square	1385 Broadway
London	New York
WC1B 3DP	NY 10018
UK	USA

www.bloomsbury.com

Bloomsbury is a registered trade mark of Bloomsbury Publishing Plc

First published 2017

British Library Cataloguing-in-Publication Data

A catalogue record for this book is available from the British Library.

ISBN: PB: 978-1-3500-4691-7
ePub: 978-1-3500-4690-0
ePDF: 978-1-3500-4692-4

Library of Congress Cataloging-in-Publication Data

A catalog record for this book is available from the Library of Congress.

Series: Modern Plays

Front cover design by Publicis Dublin
Cover image © Liam Murphy
Typeset by Mark Heslington Ltd, Scarborough, North Yorkshire

Fishamble: The New Play Company presents

Maz and Bricks

by Eva O'Connor

Cast

Maz	**Eva O'Connor**
Bricks	**Stephen Jones**

Production Team

Directed by Jim Culleton
Set and Costume Design by Maree Kearns
Lighting Design by Sinéad McKenna
Sound Design by Carl Kennedy
Production Manager   Eoin Kilkenny
Stage Manager   Tara Doolan
Dramaturg   Gavin Kostick
*Assistant Director**   Rosa Bowden
Assistant Lighting Designer   Colm McNally
Produced by Eva Scanlan

*UCD and Gaiety School of Acting placement, as part of
Fishamble's theatre company-in-association partnership at UCD

Playwright's Notes

Indented text indicates that the characters are speaking to the audience in internal monologue style. Where the text is laid out as regular dialogue they are speaking to each other.

Thanks

I would like to thank Jim, Gavin and Eva from Fishamble for their unwavering support and guidance. It's an absolute privilege to be working with such passionate people.

I would also like to thank Hildegard Ryan, Aisling O'Connor and Frances Arnold, three brilliant women who keep me on the straight and narrow.

About Fishamble: The New Play Company

Fishamble is an Olivier Award-winning, internationally acclaimed Irish theatre company, which discovers, develops and produces new work, across a range of scales. Fishamble is committed to touring throughout Ireland and internationally, and does so through partnerships and collaborations with a large network of venues, festivals and non-arts organisations.

Fishamble has earned a reputation as 'a global brand with international theatrical presence' (Irish Times), 'forward-thinking Fishamble' (New York Times), 'acclaimed Irish company' (Scotsman) and 'excellent Fishamble . . . Ireland's terrific Fishamble' (Guardian) through touring its productions to audiences in Ireland as well as to England, Scotland, Wales, France, Germany, Iceland, Croatia, Belgium, Czech Republic, Switzerland, Bulgaria, Romania, Serbia, Turkey, Finland, USA, Canada, New Zealand and Australia.

Fishamble is at the heart of new writing for theatre in Ireland, not just through its productions, but through its extensive programme of Training, Development and Mentoring schemes. These include the *New Play Clinic* and 2017 Irish Times Theatre Award nominated *Show in a Bag* which is run in partnership with Dublin Fringe Festival and Irish Theatre Institute. Each year, Fishamble typically supports 60 per cent of the writers of all new plays produced on the island of Ireland, approximately fifty-five plays per year.

Fishamble's recent, current and future productions include:

- *The Humours of Bandon* by Margaret McAuliffe (2017) on national and international tour

- *On Blueberry Hill* by Sebastian Barry (2017)

- *Charolais* by Noni Stapleton (2017) in New York

- *Inside the GPO* by Colin Murphy (2016) performed in the GPO at Easter

- *Tiny Plays for Ireland and America* by twenty-six writers (2016) at the Kennedy Center, Washington DC, and Irish Arts Center, New York, as part of *Ireland 100*

- *Mainstream* by Rosaleen McDonagh (2016) in coproduction with Project Arts Centre

- *Invitation to a Journey* by David Bolger, Deirdre Gribbin and Gavin Kostick (2016) in co-production with CoisCeim, Crash Ensemble and Galway International Arts Festival

- *Underneath* by Pat Kinevane (since 2014) winner of The Scotsman Fringe First Award and Adelaide Fringe Best Theatre Award, touring in Ireland, UK, Europe, US, Australia

- *Little Thing, Big Thing* by Donal O'Kelly (2014 – 16) winner of The Stage Award for Acting Excellence and 1st Irish Best Production Award, touring in Ireland, UK, Europe, New York, Australia

- *Silent* by Pat Kinevane (since 2011) winner of an Olivier Award, The Scotsman Fringe First Award, Herald Angel Award, Argus Angel Award, touring in Ireland, UK, Europe, US, Australia

- *Swing* by Steve Blount, Peter Daly, Gavin Kostick and Janet Moran (2014–16) touring in Ireland, UK, Europe, US, Australia and New Zealand

- *Forgotten* by Pat Kinevane (since 2007) touring in Ireland, UK, Europe, US

- *Spinning* by Deirdre Kinahan (2014) at Dublin Theatre Festival

- *The Wheelchair on My Face* by Sonya Kelly (2013–14) winner of The Scotsman Fringe First Award, touring in Ireland, UK, Europe, US

Fishamble Staff: Jim Culleton (Artistic Director), Eva Scanlan (General Manager), Gavin Kostick (Literary Manager)

Fishamble Board: Tania Banotti, Padraig Burns, Liz Davis, Peter Finnegan, Vincent O'Doherty, John O'Donnell, Siobhan O'Leary, Andrew Parkes (Chair)

Fishamble wishes to thank the following Friends of Fishamble for their invaluable support:

Alan and Rosemarie Ashe, Halsey and Sandra Beemer, Mary Banotti, Tania Banotti, Colette Bowles Breen, Padraig Burns, Maura Connolly, Ray Dolphin, John Fanagan, Barbara FitzGerald, Cora Fitzsimons, Pauline Gibney, Ann Glynn, Eithne Healy, John and Yvonne Healy, The Georganne Aldrich Heller Foundation, Gillie Hinds, Jane and Geoffrey Keating, Lisney, Richard McCullough, Stuart McLaughlin, Aidan Murphy, Liz Nugent, Lucy Nugent, Patrick Molloy, Dympna Murray, Vincent O'Doherty, Joanna Parkes, Nancy Pasley, Georgina Pollock, David and Veronica Rowe, Colleen Savage, Mary Sheerin, Grace Smith, Claudia Carroll. Thank you also to all those who do not wish to be credited.

'Ireland's terrific Fishamble', **The Guardian, 2015**

'Fishamble puts electricity in the National grid of dreams', **Sebastian Barry**

fishamble.com   facebook.com/fishamble twitter.com/fishamble

Fishamble is funded by the Arts Council and Dublin City Council. Its international touring is supported by Culture Ireland.

Acknowledgements

Thanks to the following for their help with this production: Rachel West and all at the Arts Council; Cian and Orla and everyone at Project; Louise and Marketa and everyone at Belltable, Laura and Gemma and all at the O'Reilly Theatre; everyone at 3 Great Denmark Street; and all those who have helped since this publication went to print.

Biographies

Eva O'Connor is an Irish writer and performer from Ogonnelloe, Co. Clare. During her time studying English and German at Edinburgh University (2009–13), Eva founded Sunday's Child Theatre Company, and has since written and produced five plays with the company. Eva was also selected as a member of the *Traverse 50* playwriting scheme in 2014.

In 2012 Eva won the NSDF award for Best Emerging Artist with her play *Kiss Me and You Will See How Important I Am* at the Edinburgh Fringe. Her one woman show, *My Name is Saoirse*, directed by Hildegard Ryan, won the First Fortnight Award at the Dublin Fringe 2014, an Argus Angel Award at the Brighton Fringe 2015, and the Best Theatre Award (week 3) at the Adelaide Fringe 2017. Eva also adapted *My Name is Saoirse* for RTE Radio 1, which broadcast in their Drama On One slot in April 2015.

Eva's play *Overshadowed*, directed by Hildegard Ryan, premiered at the Dublin Fringe 2015 and won the Fishamble Award for best new writing. It was subsequently performed in Project Arts at the First Fortnight Festival 2016, Theatre503 in London, Assembly Venues at the Edinburgh Fringe, and went on to tour around Ireland in October 2016.

Eva also has an MA in Theatre Ensemble from Rose Bruford Drama School in London, where she won the Jean Benedetti Award 2014 upon graduation.

Stephen Jones is from Tallaght and is a graduate of UCD. Some of his theatre credits include *DruidMurphy:* Plays by Tom Murphy, *Dubliners* at the Dublin Theatre Festival, *Alone it Stands, Stones in his Pockets, Are you there Garth? It's me Margaret,* the leading role of Keano in the hit comedy musical *I Keano, This Lime Tree Bower, Danny and Chantelle: Still here, From Eden* and the role of Thomas MacDonagh in *Signatories* which played at Kilmainham Gaol during the 1916 centenary celebrations. Film and television credits include: *Between the Canals, King of the Travellers, Scratch, Amber, Pheasant Island, Damo & Ivor, Ripper Street, The Bloody Irish, Love/Hate* and TV3's *Red Rock* as Laser Byrne. Stephen has performed in numerous radio plays for RTÉ Drama on One including the role of Christy Mahon in *The Playboy of the Western World*. Stephen is also a playwright. His play *From Eden* was the winner of the Stewart Parker Trust/BBC Northern Ireland Radio Drama Award.

Jim Culleton is the artistic director of Fishamble: The New Play Company. For Fishamble, he has directed productions which have won Olivier, The Stage, Fringe First, Herald Angel, Argus Angel, 1st Irish, Adelaide Fringe and Irish Times Theatre awards, on tour throughout Ireland, UK, Europe, Australia and the US. Current and recent productions for Fishamble include *Inside the GPO* by Colin Murphy (staged in the GPO for Easter 2016); *Invitation to a Journey* (with David Bolger, in co-production with CoisCeim, Crash Ensemble and GIAF); *Mainstream* by Rosaleen McDonagh (Project co-production); *Tiny Plays for Ireland and America* (Kennedy Center, Washington DC, and Irish Arts Center, New York, for *Ireland 100*); *Spinning* by Deirdre Kinahan (Dublin Theatre Festival); *Little Thing, Big Thing* by Donal O'Kelly (touring in Ireland, UK, Europe, US, Australia); and the multi award-winning *Forgotten, Silent* and *Underneath* by Pat Kinevane (touring to over sixty Irish venues and seventeen other countries), all three of which have just finished a run on the Abbey's Peacock stage.

He has also directed for the Abbey Theatre, Woodpecker/the Gaiety, 7:84 (Scotland), Project Arts Centre, Amharclann de hIde, Amnesty International, Tinderbox, The Passion Machine, The Ark, Second Age, RTÉ Radio 1, The Belgrade, TNL Canada, Dundee Rep Ensemble, Draíocht, Barnstorm, TCD School of Drama, Frontline Defenders, Fighting Words, Guna Nua, Origin (New York), Vessel (Australia), Little Museum of Dublin, Symphony Space/Irish Arts Center (New York) and RTÉ lyric fm. Jim has taught for NYU, NUIM, GSA, Notre Dame, TCD, UCD and Uversity.

Maree Kearns previously designed *Invitation to a Journey* for CoisCéim, Crash Ensemble, Fishamble and Galway International Arts Festival.

Other work includes *Agnes, Pageant and Faun/As You Are* (CoisCéim); *Opera Briefs* (RIAM); *Monsters, Dinosaurs and Ghosts* (Peacock); *Moll* (Gaiety Theatre); *Desire Under The Elms* (Corn Exchange); *These Halcyon Days* (Edinburgh Fringe First 2013); *Moment* (Landmark/Tall Tales); *Far Away From Me* and *Zoe's Play* (The Ark); *In the Next Room or The Vibrator Play, Troilus and Cressida* (the Lir Academy); *Hamlet, King Lear, Romeo and Juliet, Macbeth* and *Dancing at Lughnasa* (Second Age); *Anglo the Musical* (Verdant); *The Factory Girls* (Millennium Forum); *Faith and Goddess of Liberty* (Gúna Nua); *Plasticine* (CorcaDorca); and *The Dead School* and *Observe the Sons of*

Ulster Marching Towards the Somme (Irish Times Best Set Design 2009) (Nomad Network). Maree lectures in theatre design in the Drama Department of Trinity College and is the MFA Design Course Director in the Lir Academy of Dramatic Art in Dublin.

Sinéad McKenna has previously designed *The Gist of It* for Fishamble and *Invitation to a Journey* for CoisCéim, Crash Ensemble, Fishamble and Galway International Arts Festival. Other recent designs include: *Grace Jones – the Musical of My Life* (Blinder Films); *Prodijig* (Cork Opera House); *Agnes, Pageant, Swept* (Cois Ceim); *Private Lives* (2017); *Beckett/Pinter/Friel Festival, Juno and the Paycock, A Month in the Country, The Gigli Concert, The Mariner, The Price, An Ideal Husband* and *Private Lives* (Gate Theatre); *Uncle Vanya* and *Richard III* (West Yorkshire Playhouse); *The Wake, Othello, Aristocrats, Quietly, Alice in Funderland, The Plough and the Stars, 16 Possible Glimpses, The Burial at Thebes, Howie the Rookie, Finders Keepers* (Abbey Theatre, Dublin); *New Electric Ballroom* (Druid Theatre Company/ international tour); *Howie the Rookie* (Best Lighting Design Irish Theatre Awards), *Greener, October, Last Days of the Celtic Tiger, Blackbird* (Landmark Productions); *Dubliners* (Corn Exchange); *Famished Castle, Travesties, The Importance of Being Earnest, Improbable Frequency* (New York Drama Desk Best Lighting Design for a Musical nomination 2009); *The Parker Project, Life is a Dream, Attempts on Her Life* and *Dream of Autumn* (Rough Magic). She has also worked with Decadent, Gare St Lazare, Corn Exchange, THISISPOPBABY, Siren, The Lyric, Second Age, Performance Corporation, Semper Fi, Guna Nua. Operas include *Don Giovanni* (OTC); *La Traviata* (Malmo Opera House); *The Rape of Lucretia* (IYO); *The Magic Flute, The Marriage of Figaro* (Opera Theatre Company) and *A Midsummer Night's Dream* (Opera Ireland).

Carl Kennedy trained at Academy of Sound in Dublin. He has previously worked with Fishamble: The New Play Company on *Inside the GPO* by Colin Murphy and *Little Thing Big Thing* by Donal O'Kelly, both directed by Jim Culleton. He has worked as a composer/sound designer with venues and companies including The Abbey, The Gaiety, Decadent, ANU Productions, HOME Manchester, Prime Cut, Theatre Lovett, HotForTheatre, Rough Magic, The Lyric Theatre Belfast, Gúna Nua, Loose Canon, Peer to Peer, Siren, Broken Crow, Randolf SD and Theatre Makers. He has been nominated three times for the Irish Times Theatre Award for Best Sound Design. He also composes music and sound design for

TV and video games. Game titles include *Curious George, Curious about Shapes and Colors, Jelly Jumble, Too Many Teddies, Dino Dog* and *Leonardo and his Cat*. TV credits include sound design for *16 Letters* (Independent Pictures/RTÉ) and SFX editing and foley recording for *Centenary* (RTÉ).

Gavin Kostick works as Literary Manager of Fishamble with writers for theatre through development for production, scripts readings, mentorship programmes and a variety of courses and workshops. Gavin is also a playwright who has written over twenty plays which have been produced in Ireland and internationally. As a performer he performed Joseph Conrad's *Heart of Darkness: Complete*, a six hour show in Dublin and London. In all of these areas he has gained multiple awards.

Eva Scanlan returned to Fishamble: The New Play Company in 2016 as General Manager and Producer. Current and recent work includes Fishamble's award-winning Pat Kinevane Trilogy on tour in Ireland and internationally, *The Humours of Bandon* by Margaret McAuliffe, *Inside the GPO* by Colin Murphy, *Tiny Plays for Ireland and America* at the Kennedy Center in Washington DC and the Irish Arts Center in New York, and *Swing* by Steve Blount, Peter Daly, Gavin Kostick and Janet Moran on tour in Ireland, the UK, and Australia. Eva produces *The 24 Hour Plays: Dublin* at the Abbey Theatre in Ireland (2012–17), in association with the 24 Hour Play Company, New York, and has worked on the 24 Hour Plays on Broadway and the 24 Hour Musicals at the Gramercy Theatre. Previously, she was Producer of terraNOVA Collective in New York (2012–15), where she produced *terraNOVA Rx: Four Plays in Rep* at IRT Theater, the soloNOVA Arts Festival, the Groundworks New Play Series, *Woman of Leisure and Panic* (FringeNYC), *P.S. Jones and the Frozen City,* among other projects. Other Irish work includes producing *At The Ford* for RISE Productions, written by Gavin Kostick and directed by Bryan Burroughs, and as line producer for *I'm Your Man* by Mark Matthew Palmer and Phillip McMahon for Project Arts Centre and THISISPOPBABY, both as part of the Dublin Theatre Festival 2016.

Maz and Bricks

Characters

Maz
Bricks

On the Luas. **Bricks** *is on the phone. He has a little girl's* Frozen *rucksack on his knee.* **Maz** *is sitting opposite him making a placard.*

Bricks You well, Batman ? You still at it? Keepin' the session lit wha?

You poor lad! (*To* **Maz**.) He's weepin' cos someone just opened the curtains. We don't call him Batman for nothing, hangin' in a cave is his natural habitat. Nah man, I slipped out round three, I was proper sensible last night, so I was. How many times do I have to tell ya? I'm a fucking pioneer Batty. I'm clean as a whistle. (*Whistles tunefully.*) I wasn't about to do yokes the night before I have Yas, now was I?! Well you're an irresponsible prick.

Oh I had a laugh alright, don't you worry. Your wan Jessica provided me with *ample* entertainment (**Bricks** *winks at* **Maz**.) if you know what I mean.

Jessica, Jacintha. I'm useless with names, ya, yer one in the sparkly dress. Jesus the state of her, she was like a walking disco ball, I was doing everyone a favour by taking it off. She was giving your guests a collective headache. She was a tidy ride, so she was, unfortunate face, but a force of nature in the sack. Ah sure, the chubby ones always surprise ya.

Pause.

What? Say that again, I think I'm after mishearing ya, I'm on the Luas, Batty, the bad signal is scrambling ya . . . She's Lara's cousin? You're not fucking serious. She shagged me on purpose, the sparkly cunt! It's a fucking set up.

Why the fuck did you fail to mention that last night you Charlie fiend? Of course it's your fault. Well maybe if you weren't out of your nut on horse pesticide then you might have noticed I was about to ride her, and tipped me off.

Fuck it, you know what, Batty, I'm a young man in my sexual prime and I can shag anyone I like. As Britney would say if she was still alive, that's my prerogative.

Fuckin' hell, Batty, get over yourself would ya. It's a fuckin' comedown. There's worse things than a bit of natural light. Sure you could have a micro penis, or OR you could have shagged your psycho-ex-birds's cousin. Does that put things in perspective for ya?

Look, Bat, I have to bounce. I'm getting filthies off your one across from me. I think she's trying to draw me, sure who can blame her, I'm a fine figure of a man. But you know me, can't sit still for a nano second. I'm just an animated kinda guy. Wha? I'm the Luas, with an artiste. Ya ya. Tell me about it, I hope she's doing my good side – (*To* **Maz**.) I've an awful unsymmetrical face love, can you make my lazy eye behave itself? Lara's gonna skin me alive when I collect Yas, I might as well get me portrait done before she finishes me off. Something to remember me by. Good luck, Batty. Get a few cans into you, be grand.

Was I fierce loud on the phone there, was I? (*In an obnoxious whisper.*) Sorry! You wouldn't believe the personal drama I've got going on. I was at a small dinner party type affair last night and I'm after accidentally sleeping with me ex's cousin –

Maz   I'm not drawing you.

Bricks   Ah don't be embarrassed love, sure I know I make a pretty picture.

Maz   I said I'm not drawing you.

Bricks   That's fine, love (*He winks.*) Sure we'll say no more so.

Maz   Wow.

Bricks   Good jaw line I know. My mam's side. The O'Donnells. Cheek bones to die for. Real Roman looking.

Maz   I meant like wow it's been a while since I met some one this wildly inappropriate.

Bricks   Inappropriate? Careful now love, that sounded dangerously like an insult. Rub me up the wrong way and

I'll hop off at the next stop and take this (**Bricks** *gestures to his face*) with me.

Maz Hop off when ever you like.

Bricks Ah but you'd miss me.

Maz Me and everyone else here would have withdrawal symptoms, I'm sure.

Bricks Your art would suffer.

Maz I'm not making art.

Bricks Sure isn't self-deprecation the sign of a good artist. Give us a look. Go on go on go on. Don't worry if you haven't quite nailed my nose, I broke it when I was six, leapt off the roof with a bed sheet for a parachute, and it's never been the same since. It'll probably take you a few goes.

Maz *turns the placard she has been working on around. It reads 'Justice for Eimear'.*

Maz It's for the pro choice protest.

Bricks Wooahhh . . . I don't want my face on some kind of abortion advert.

Maz A nineteen-year-old girl called Eimear Colgan died yesterday because she needed an abortion and she didn't have access to one. And this afternoon there's a demo to mark her death, and to pressure our backwards government to change the law. Your face is in no way involved.

Bricks The dirty A-word. I'd keep your voice down if I was you, there's old people on this train, they might get offended.

Maz You think abortion is an offensive word?

Bricks I'm not easily offended, love. I've thick skin, so I do, thick as a rhino. But you have to respect the OAPs.

Maz Abortion, abortion, ABORTION.

Bricks   An artist and a rebel. A woman of many talents.

Maz   There's nothing rebellious about saying the word 'abortion'.

Bricks   Ah but it's a slippery slope. One day you're going round saying the word, the next you're *having* one.

Maz   The girl who died yesterday would still be alive if she had been allowed to have one when she needed it.

Bricks   That's real sad, love, I heard it on Joe Duffy, and it sounded proper tragic. Thing is, I've a daughter, Yasmine's her name, she's just gone four and she is the best thing that ever happened to me. Fucking apple of me eye, so she is, and speaking as a father, I just can't get behind the whole thing.

Maz   Loving your daughter, and legalising abortion are completely separate issues. Today is difficult enough as it is, and I just want to finish this placard and –

Bricks   I'm interrupting your art, I'm sorry. I could talk for Ireland. I'll leave you to it.

Pause.

Bricks   You had an abortion, didn't you?

Maz   What's it to you?

Bricks   I knew it! There was something about your angry scribbling. Look at you, all up on your high horse, making art about your trauma!

Maz   This conversation I'm having with you is the most traumatic part of the entire thing, by a fucking country mile.

Bricks   Country mile? I'm not sure what bogger county you hail from, love, but you're in Dublin now and we measure in kilometres. Like the French. We're very modern, so we are, us Dubs.

Maz   Sounds about right. Modernise the road signs. Legalise gay marriage. Just don't touch the sacred eighth amendment.

Bricks Amendment she says. Are you American? You can't be American with that culchie accent on ya.

Maz I love a good abortion, so I do. Normally I have one in the morning over a nice strong espresso. Then later on round 3pm I'll start to crave another. I have my last one whilst watching Netflix, just before I go to sleep. Obviously flying over and back to England multiple times a day is a bit of a pain in the vagina, but when they eventually legalise abortion here, probably in the next 500 years, then I'll be laughing.

Bricks You're sick in the head do ya know that. This is a life and death situation, and you're taking the piss.

Maz You're right it is life or death. People are literally dying because we don't have access to abortion. Another woman is dead. Eimear Colgan is dead. It's a joke. It's a sick joke. You have to laugh as they say. Ha ha ha ha ha!

Bricks Look, I didn't mean to provoke ya. I didn't realise you felt so strongly about it. Did you know her, this Eimear one?

Maz No, but I feel like I did. You're right, I did have an abortion. And I had to travel in secret to get it done, and for months afterwards I didn't tell a soul, until I thought I was gonna explode if I held it in any longer. So now I just tell people. Fuck it, I tell anyone who will listen.

Bricks Wow, and I thought I was an over-sharer.

Maz I even tell strangers on the Luas, who call me sick in the head.

Bricks Ah, that's a term of endearment.

Maz Eimear wasn't well enough or well off enough to travel, and now she's dead. It could have been me. And that's why I'm making this placard, and that's why I'm going on the march.

Bricks   Jesus, you don't beat around the bush, do ya? I suppose you artists are like tha'. Always pushing boundaries. Making pensioners uncomfortable.

Maz   Am I making you uncomfortable?

Bricks   Nah. Me uncomfortable? Nah.

Maz   I just thought, since you're blushing that . . . maybe ?

Bricks   That's just me tanned complexion.

Maz   So you don't have a problem with my placard?

Bricks   Listen love. Unlike you, I'm a parent. Like I said, it's cos of me daughter, you know . . . that I'm on the fence about the ethics of it.

Maz   The ethics of what? ABORTION.

Bricks   Christ alive. There's absolutely no need to raise your voice like that. This is *public* transport.

Silence.

Are you haunted by it? By your . . . *abortion.*

Maz   What I'm haunted by is that girl dying yesterday, that's what I'm haunted by.

Maz *continues to colour in her placard furiously. Suddenly her marker stops working.*

Maz   Shit.

Bricks   Did you go outside the lines? Hate that. Drives Yas insane. She's a little perfectionist, so she is.

Maz *shakes her marker, which is no longer working.*

Bricks   It's given up on ya?

Bricks *reaches into the* Frozen *rucksack and takes out a marker and hands it to* **Maz**.

Bricks   Here. Take it. It's Yasmine's. She'd want you to have it. You remind me of her, how headstrong you are. Ye'd get on well. She's a brilliant artist, Yas is. Only four and I tell you what, her stuff's better than most of the shite you see in the National Gallery.

Maz   Thank her for me.

Bricks   You should thank her yourself. We're going to the zoo if ya fancy it? Feed the penguins instead of going on a death march?

Maz *glares at him.*

Bricks   I'm only messing. Sure the zoo is a rip off anyway. Seventeen fifty for an adult. Can you believe that? To see a few bare arse monkeys and a depressed rhino.

Maz   Daylight robbery.

Bricks   Sure, I might not even make it to the zoo. I have to face my ex first, Yasmine's mam. I'll be an endangered species as soon as she hears about me shenanigans last night. I'm after making the small faux pas of sleeping –

Maz   – with her cousin. I know. I heard.

Bricks   You're a funny one, d'ya know that . . . what's your name?

Maz   Maz.

Bricks   Maz, I'm Bricks. I like you, you know that. I know we've only just met, but you're my favourite abortionist.

* * *

Maz   I'm first off the Luas and gagging to go. The Irish for 'speed', my absolute hole. I've been sitting on that metal can for what feels like a whole lifetime, flailing around for a lifeline of any description, considering alighting early to escape. Yer man, Bricks he called himself, apt, he's probably as thick as one, sing songing his life story in my face like we were alone, 'a disgrace', I heard an aul one mumble across from me as he swore, but in spite of myself, I half liked him. Half. No more.

Abbey Street, and town is packed, bursting at the concrete seams. Admittedly it seems like most people are march bound but I can't muster solidarity with masses moving this fucking slow, and yes she's dead, but this is not a funeral, why are people moving like they came to show their kowtowed respect, not their fucking anger rising in me, coming up my throat, bile and heart burn like. I need a Rennie to remedy this, 'breeeeeathe' I say out loud, inadvertently into the ear of a woman in front of me. I tickle her with my panicked breath, that's how close I am to her freckly neck and she backwards glances me like 'thanks for the reminder love'.

Placard in hand I'm armed. I've landed in Dublin and I'm scoping the vibes. 'Try me' I think, 'just try my patience'. It's shrivelled already, it's papery thin, I hate crowds, but I brace myself and worm my way in.

Bricks   Town is cattle mart rammed, not that I've ever even clapped eyes on a cattle in my city boy life. It's quite a sight, match day for feminists, like the evil Corconians have just beat us in the final. Last time that happened I painted the Cork colours on the floor of the urinal. Bloodied red banners, screaming, flags, tears even, and obscene amount of swag, an apocalyptic crush. Dublin it doesn't suit you, all this and shoving and push looks wrong on ya.

I'm in no rush so I amble behind the droves. I always leave too much time to get to Lara's place, punctual to the excess, to assure, to impress upon her I take the parenting serious, like. And I do alright?! Though I've a feeling no premature

arrival will quite cancel out last night's faux pas,
I'm an unbelievable spa. I feel sick, I'm regretting
this morning's six Weetabix. I offer up a quick
prayer to the blessed Virgin 'you're looking well
Mary up above, I'd properly love ya forever if you
could do us a favour, and keep an eye on me
bowels, they're brewing and stewing, and let's just
say doing things I don't want them to. Just buy me
an hour before they explode you're an absolute
dote. Amen.'

I've half a mind to hop back on the red line, go
crawling back to Batty's cave for a few de-stressing
breakfast lines. But I need to see Yas, ergo I have to
face her mother. I'm a born and bred numpty.
There were a million other mots to ride at last
night's gaff but then again, only three of them were
old enough to bang legal like. But seriously, her
cousin of all fucking people. No more shagging
and bragging for me, it's sad but next time I'll be
forced to ask for some ID.

Maz   I pick up the pace, I'm ansty, addled I'll be late,
and I'm timeless. My phone as usual is a little bitch,
six minutes fast or slow, I can never think which.
And I'm aware the crowd's headed for the one
assembly point, but I'm anxious, I'm all out of
joint, stressing that I'll miss it. That all the twisted
rage inside me that bus, trained and Luased me to
here, that all the toxic fear I've stored up, boarded
up inside me will eat me alive before I reach the
frontline. I've been up since six and time is playing
tricks on my mind. I'm wrecked, my organs feel
hot inside from how tired I am, and yet I'm wired,
I am.

Bricks   I snails pace it over towards Gardiner Street. I'm
gagging for a smoke so hard I've a death wish. I
tap a fag off a lad next to me. I swoon with the

drag I savour the air. I'm meant to be off them but
my efforts are futile. I don't care about toxic black
tar lining my lungs. Am I zen or a realist or just
coked up numb?

I'm sure cancer will get me, malignant and stealthy,
invade my bronchioles and many other holes,
but I've about as much interest in dying healthy as
I do in taking up cricket.

I'm approaching Lara's flat now, and I whip out a
Vaseline tin, and lather up my lips before I head in.
A protective layer of petroleum jelly, soothes the
scabs on my lips. I swallow a bit. Maybe it'll ease the
knot in my belly. When I get to Lara's door I'm not
gonna lie, I'd absolutely love, I'd pay the bleak
concrete floor a fiver to gobble me up. Nom nom
nom, three chews I'd be gone.

Maz   I'm wound up bound up for the front of the
march. My mouth's lined with sandpaper, I'm
parched. There's pushing at my every limb
swelling, no telling when it will let up. I'm sweating
I'm het up, I whip out a can. Sigh it open in my left
hand, and freeze time with four gulps. I'm
engulfed in liquid relief but it fizzes out, it's
teasingly brief.

Bricks   The anger in Lara's eyes terrifies me. It's the size
of two small countries. Her black pupils are
swimming with it, brimming with it, hatred. Or
something akin to it.

'You' she says, barely audible. Laudable, applaud-
able I suppose that she's not shouting. Yet. I'm
ready, I'm set to defend myself. Calmly. I'm a
sensible man, and my plan is to fight fire with a fire
extinguisher. 'Look love,' I'll say. 'Last night I did
not go looking for a shag, I was at Batty's,
sober as a bar a soap, aimless, borderline sad, that's

how lonely I was and your cousin wandered into a bed that I happened to be snoozing in.' I'll omit that I was perusing, proper prowling the place, schmoozing anyone who would give me the time of night.

'I give you an inch and you take a mile.'

'Ah come on Lara, it's been a while.'

'We're on a "break".'

'My mistake, I didn't realise you still owned me.'

'You rode my cousin?'

'I didn't have a bull's notion you were related.'

'We're identical, we've carbon copy blue eyes!'

'Yer nothing alike, she's twice your size.'

I want to add the words 'and she's fuckin' crosseyed!' but I swallow them back. She starts to laugh.

'I'm here for Yas. Let's just park this.'

'Park this?! You have a fling with my spitting image cousin, outta the dozens of people you coulda chosen. And you think I'm gonna let it go?'

'I'm just asking you not to make a show, in front of Yas.'

'You want me to conceal your man slut behavior, so she'll worship you, think that you're her fuckin' savior?'

'Lara, let's be adult about this.'

'Adult as in sleeping around? You after all these years I thought you were sound. Irresponsible, and fucked up, a waste of space but ultimately good. But you run off and revenge fuck at the first chance you could. You're the most selfish man I've ever met. Have you ever heard of a thing called respect?!'

I'm totting up in my bleeding brain how long it's gonna take till she's sufficiently shamed me and I'm free to go.

'It was a one night stand.'

'You're a pathetic excuse for a man, you know that? You need to look in the mirror and examine what you see, cos as far as I'm concerned you're not fit to be a dad right now.'

'Not fit to be a dad! I'm a better parent than you. You're pathetic! You're fucking sad.'

'Piss off, and don't even think of taking Yas. And when you've sorted your shit out, when you manage to do a single thing that doesn't involve you being number one, then come crawling back. And I'll see what can be done.'

'Lara, do not blackmail me! Can you not see the damage you're doing here, we have to be civil for Yas's sake, and if you're waiting for me to change my mind and take you back it's not –'

'You deserve a fucking smack!'

Maz   The taste of the air is wrong in my mouth. All that aer úr propaganda the tourist board sprouts is a lot a bullshit. No wonder we're all so repressed, so bluish pale. I want to spit it out before I choke, it's rancid and stale. Deceptively mild, inoffensively meek, harmless as a field of bleating, dyed sheep. But this Irish air fosters the saddest events. A hundred hard won years spent hashtag 'was it for this?' *This* doesn't feel like freedom to me. I glance back at the statue, yer man near the bridge. Is it James Connolly? Or Joyce, or Larkin or maybe

Parnell? They're all the same, they're all arrogant
men, I can't even tell. It's Daniel O'Connell. Ya I
know alright. I'd tear them all down given a choice,
the men on their pedestals, safe in their
stone, phallic and towering, erect and alone.
Running this town, overseeing the city. Stop
smiling O'Connell. Today won't be pretty.

Bricks   When Lara's rant finally ceases, oh sweet Jesus,
from down the darkened hallway behind her
comes Yas in her pyjamas still, the *Frozen* ones, of
course, and all I want is to rewind. Because Yas, my
baby, is clearly upset and she's too precious, too
small, too young yet, thank God, to fully grasp that
I wouldn't waste another micro second of my life
on Lara, if she wasn't her mother. But there's a
look on Yas's face that tells me the penny is
dropping and she's dancing with distress now,
crying, hopping on the spot. It makes my heart
bleed. 'I want Da to come in and play with me.'

Maz   Parnell Square finally and I feel a hand on my
back. I swivel 180° 'what?!' I'm on the attack, and
when I see who it is, I'm so taken aback I'm
speechless. Lucinda McNally, a woman I haven't
seen or heard of since I left home three years ago.
And on one hand the time has flown, and on the
other I feel like I've lived a lifetime on my own.

Lucinda was my baby-sitter when Mam couldn't
afford anyone else in our one horse town. Do
Lally'd mind me for zilch, her services were free on
the bizarre condition she could teach me, I shit you
not, to garden. And here she is at this sprawling
rally. None other than hippy Do Lally.

'Maz,' she says, 'Maz, it's me . . .'

Well obviously Lally, that I can see, you're up in my
face, I'm not about to mistake you were the one

and only skinny dipping acid tripping, urine
sipping hippie in my childhood. I remember you.

'Hi Lucinda.'

Bricks   Lara's looking at me like she wishes I was dead.
'You heard what I said. Now fuck off.'

'Don't swear at me.'

'Oh please. It's not rocket science, Bricks; your
actions have repercussions. This discussion is over.'

Maz   Lucinda helped me in unspeakable ways, I owe her
my life, my debt to her is a size and shape I can
never repay. And I'm sweating at the sight of her,
this willowy woman from my past. 'Open your
mouth and say a fucking thank you', a voice hisses
inside my mind. 'After the infinite kindness she
showed you, now you've gone mute?'

A smile stretches across her lips.

'It's good to see you.'

'Say thank you.' I dare myself, but no words come.
She steps away. We're done. No resentment. She
knows I need to be alone today. But something hits
me as she backs away. I can make out the trace, the
underline of a faint bump, contours of a baby to be.

'You're expecting?' I say. My words surprise even
me.

She nods and I can tell that she's brimming with
pride. This child is already the apple of her eye.
And what a statement to make with your baby to
be. The power of an unborn child under a faded
'Repeal' t-shirt. It makes me almost believe that all
this might change.

'Congratulations,' I manage and I mean it. I'm
happy for her with all the blood in my veins. But as

I turn to go I clock what I think is . . . pain? In Do
Lally's eyes, she blinks. I think she almost cries as
we part. Cos we're all here, cos we've been
wronged. We've been daylight robbed, the place is
thronged, half the nation's on the streets, we're
ranting, mourning with our feet.

Bricks I'm craving Yas like I'm coming off a hard drug.
I'm desperate to hug her, to hold her squishy body
in my arms til I'm warm completely from her
perfect radiator skin. My breaths are coming
shallow and fast, I need a blast of my inhaler,
maybe I'm hallucinating, losing it, but the loopy
twisted font of Anto's tattoo swims into my brain.
His fucking lame, hippy slogan inked across his
white blue skin 'This too shall pass'.

The last thing I said to him, meaning the pain, not
thinking that the same would be true of his twenty-
two-year-old life. And I'd have sold my soul to go
instead, to fight the hellbent demon inside his
tortured head.

My phone beeps, practically leaps out of my
pocket, and I hope with every ounce of me for an
apology from a sheepish Lara. For a 'Come and
take Yas to the zoo. She's inconsolable and she only
wants you.' But it's Mam.

'I can't believe we're a year without him. Promise
me you'll be at the church tomorrow. M. x'

Alright, Anto, 'this too shall pass', but I'm not
going to that fuckin' mass.

Maz We're a body of bodies hot with angry heat. A
million shifting stamping feet. We're a host of
unfixed molecules, bumping and grinding our
teeth in worn-down rage. We're all elbows in each
other's ribs, sweat and skin, a crush akin to that
time I nearly died at a Girls Aloud gig to *The Sound*

of the Underground, thinking 'so this is what dying feels like', feet flailing miles from ground. As the march begins to move, I can feel it in my waters, it's gonna kick off soon. It's the tip of the iceberg about to sink a ship this very afternoon.

The last time I was in this neck of the city's woods, there was a herd of animal-lovers camped outside the GPO, pushing, shoving their vegan slogans down the throats of passers-by. With their petitions, battery chicken photos, war cries, 'Go vegan and save the lambs, their tasty blood is on your hands!'

But today the Cowspiracy campaigners, the puppy eyed complainers, have been ousted by a strong cohort of 'Pro Life' reads one placard in bold. The sight of it feels like a physical blow.

Bricks   I'm coming up Talbot Street, aimless, reeling from defeat, I'm doing deep breathing, staring at my feet until the noise from O'Connell Street seizes my attention. Till now I had forgotten about the feminazi demonstration. The crowd ahead is sprawling, bawling, chanting things I can't make out. There's enough anger between them to rocket them to the moon and back, and it's at this point I should probably call it quits, slack off, and then about a hundred yards from the spire, I see her. Like some kind of desert mirage, your one from the Luas. She's camouflaged in the crowd but I know her from behind, the shape of her, not just her arse alright, imprinted on my mind.

Maz   'Protect the life of an unborn child!', heads snap back like shots have been fired, it takes a while before the crowd locates the shrill anti-choice voice. In my mind's eye an emergency flare has shot up, we're bathed in its glow, an explosion, and for a split haired second there's complete silence, the air is still, it's pregnant with violence. Or is it just me?

Bricks   Like the shite car without the 'da' Maz she was called. She's floating, jostling in a sea of heads, and I know I should about turn but instead, I embark on a fairly reckless mission, like my feet have given themselves full permission, to close the gap between me and this stranger. As I get close to her, it's a full on thrill, my eyes trained on her back like she's a target and it's shoot to kill. 'Desist,' Anto used to say when I'd get riled up, I can hear him, with me somehow, like he always is, and I throw a wink to the sky, 'Desist me eye.'

Maz   And the crowd shifts towards the source of the hate, and I'm shoving through bodies, hell-bent on getting to the front line. I can't wait. This is not the time and place for holding back, I want to smack bang up against walls, the culprit of their bullshit cries, I want to pull punches, and serve up black eyes.

Bricks   And I've almost lost her in the mass uproar. She's diving and darting into the eye of the storm and I'm straining to see her. I stand on tip toe and she's up in the face of a line of cops, she's spitting and screeching. I knew this one was highly strung but she's lost it, she's flipped her lid. If she's not careful she'll be lifted. And I've a knee-jerk reaction that says I should intervene. Step in before this manic queen of protest does something she'll regret.

Maz   And if it isn't the keepers of the peace. Our faux-friendly joke of a police force between us and them. And the guards are all 'settle down now please, let's keep it calm'. It's beyond me how I'm meant to keep my head when a young woman is freshly dead and anti-choice fools are abusing me from across a row of 'All cops are bastards!'

Bricks   Who knew you could care about someone you
chatted to for five Luas minutes about their protest
art. Either this is the start of the rest of my life or
I'm gonna die at the hand of a mob of abortionists.

Maz   I spot a stone on the kerb, a perfect shaped thing
of greyish round. I'm physically drawn to it, now
that I've found it, clapped eyes on its form, or
maybe it found me, I'm buzzing, I'm hyped, I'm
half guilty. With the thought of what I know I'll do
next.

Maz *picks up a stone and is about to fling it towards the anti-choice
protesters.* **Bricks** *appears from behind her and grabs her.*

Maz   Get your fucking hand off me, you pig! Let go of me!

Bricks *releases her.*

Maz   What the fuck?!

Bricks   Surprise!

Maz   What the hell do you think you're doing? Jesus. I
thought you were . . .

Bricks *oinks.*

Maz   Fuck you.

Bricks   Ah come on, every one loves a good cop
impersonation. Sometimes I think I could have been one, in
real life. If they weren't such cunts.

Maz   How dare you lay a finger on me! You are a complete
stranger –

Bricks   Ah now love, we are hardly strangers.

Maz   You just attacked me!

Bricks   Eh, you were the one doing the attacking.

Maz   No, I was exercising my right to protest. And you
sneak up behind me, and drag me down an alleyway?

Bricks   You were about to stone a granny!

Maz   Ya, who fucking deserved it.

Bricks   You were this close to being lifted! You owe me your freedom, and now you're abusing me?!

Maz   Have you any idea how out of line you are? You're a fucking creep, sneaking up behind me like that. Christ, what is wrong with you? You're as bad as that disgusting crowd back there.

Bricks   That's harsh.

Maz   Is it? You were pro-life yourself the last time we met.

Bricks   Well, I'm not any more. I changed me mind. I'm pro-death since two minutes ago. Are you happy now?

Maz   Thrilled to bits.

Bricks   They're hardly pro-life anyway. If yer one is dead that's a bit of a contradiction.

Maz   He's catching on.

Bricks   I'm a quick learner. Am I out of the dog house now?

Maz *glares at him.*

Bricks   I am! Praise be to sweet baby Jesus! I saw that flicker of a smile.

Maz   I'm not smiling.

Bricks   You are so.

Maz   How is this a smile?

Bricks   Not on your face, but in your eyes! A cheeky glimmer. Wait?

Bricks *pulls a face at* **Maz**. *She smiles involuntarily.*

Bricks   Yes!

Maz   You're fucking ridiculous.

Bricks   And you're smiling!

Maz   So you decided to come to the death march?

Bricks   Ya, there was a slight change of plan with the zoo.
It, eh, got cancelled.

Maz   So you decided to stalk me instead?

Bricks   Ah, don't flatter yourself.

Maz   Well you hardly just randomly bumped into me.

Bricks   Exactly. Nail on the head there, love. I was just
demonstrating away, so I was, minding my own business,
next thing I spot you losing your shit. And I have experience
with the cops, you may not think it looking at me, but I do,
and they can be delicate fuckin' situations, so I intervened
ASAP and got you outta the danger zone.

Maz   Why did the zoo get cancelled?

Bricks   The weather.

Maz   The sun's shining.

Bricks   Exactly. Yas gets terrible sun burn. Can't be out in it
without a brolly. Nah. It's me ex. Won't even let me see my
own daughter. Can you believe that? Slept with someone I
shouldn't have and suddenly I'm not fit to be a dad.

Maz   So let me get this straight. Your ex is withholding your
kid cos you can't keep your dick in your pants? That's a
really tragic story but I'm struggling to see what it has to do
with me.

Bricks   Nothing. Now that I think about. Absolutely
nothing. I'll fuck off now.

Bricks *turns to walk away.*

Maz   Wait. Bricks . . . As in bricks and mortar?

Bricks   I flung one through a window when I was twelve,
and it stuck. The name, not the brick.

Maz   Bet your teachers came down on you like a ton of . . .

Bricks   That's pathetic.

Maz   You're pathetic.

Bricks   Look, flinging that brick got me in a lot of trouble. That's why I stopped you throwing that stone. I thought I was doing you a favour, alright?

Maz   Sound.

Bricks   We've veered off and we're headed down Abbey Street, tracing the tracks of our star-crossed tram meeting. I'm not really sure what the plan is, or what this highly-strung one's all about. But I'm not about to look a gift horse in the mouth. She's softer now, less aggro somehow. We fall into step, my legs longer than hers by a country mile, and the pair of us say nothing for a while. And I've a giddiness in my stomach pit, not like earlier when I was sure I'd be sick, just enough to indicate I think I like this girl, a bit. Kind of.

Maz   Look, how I acted back there . . . It was just a heat of the moment thing. I didn't mean to . . .

Bricks   Die pensioners die! Die pensioners die!

Maz   I shouldn't have risen to them, I know. It's not about them. But today of all days? It makes me sick. Did ya see the ninety-year-old with a plastic fetus on a stick. Where do they even get those things from? Do they order them off E-bay or what?

Bricks   OAPs are very tech savvy these days, love, you should know that. This is mad isn't it. Us. Just hanging out in town. Like mates. Very random.

Maz   So we're mates now?

Bricks   Course we are. Sure we go way back.

Maz   I'm not sure how this situation has arisen, I'm dizzy
still from the heat of this off the scales, off the
fucking rails afternoon. I've lost my placard and
picked up this cocky bastard, this lurker in the
shadows, shirker of responsibility. I don't even
want to know the story with his daughter. It's
fraughter with tension than he'll admit. There's a
real danger that this head-the-ball stranger has a
few screws loose. But on a day like today I'm pretty
sure I do too. And the words spew out my lips
before I think them through.

Maz   I'm parched. Do you fancy a drink?

                         * * *

Bricks   We're in a bar now, a dingy Capel Street joint, and
she makes it clear she's gagging for a pint. I'd
murder one too, I'm thirsty as an eckied racehorse,
but I know this day will only get worse, if I crumble
and cave to the devil's sauce. And although an
hour ago I was dangerously close to getting
absolutely scaldy pissed, the day took a twist, for
the better, miraculously and I'm stable again. Just
about able again to see the merit in ordering Club
Orange, rather than seven shots of straight spiced
rum.

Bricks *goes up to the bar to order a drink.*

Bricks   'Heineken and a Club Orange please buddy.'

         'No bother.'

         The barman is a greying aul lad with bushy side
         burns, visible when he side turns.

         'Mental out there, is it?'

         'Busy enough on the streets alright.'

         'Like the fucking 1916 circus all over again.'

'Never a dull moment.'

'It's terrible sad, isn't it. That Eimear one. If you ask me they should get on with it and legalise the thing. We all had our doubts about the gay marriage, but sure the world didn't end. When young ones are dyin' it's a sad state of affairs.'

He's the type you might think would be backwards in his views. The news that he's up for it too, legal abortion in Eireann, it's pretty apparent that I had my head in the sky or buried deep in the sands of time. Not the foggiest notion that women's lives were on the line. And if this scruffy publican is in the know then maybe I should just take the plunge and give this abortion thing a go.

Maz   I don't fucking know what I'm doing here with this Bricks lad. Drinking with him is the weirdest, wildest idea I've had in a long time. I suppose I hoped he'd take my mind off a march that I couldn't handle. That he'd give me a taster, a sample of the real Dublin's fair city, distract me from this god-awful, shitty day. I glance up at the bar and see him chatting away. The barman laughs as Bricks gives him a wink. I settle in and think 'fingers crossed he won't murder me after a single drink.'

Bricks *returns from the bar carrying a Club Orange for himself and a pint for* **Maz**.

Maz   You're not drinking?

Bricks   Nah, I'm being good, practising for Lent.

Maz   You're not gonna be offended if I down this are you?

Maz   You're an alcoholic?

Bricks   And you're an abortionist.

Maz   Let's call it quits. When did you give up?

Bricks   A year ago tomorrow. Cos of me brother. I'd come in pissed out of me tree, every night of the week, smash up me mam's ornaments, kick over the cat litter. Me brother, Anto, he'd just piss himself laughing. He'd lie on the couch in convulsions at how pathetic I was, playing the big man. So now whenever I feel like a drink, I imagine him laughing at me, and I inhale a Club Orange instead.

Maz   Good for you. Sounds like your brother did you a favour.

Bricks   I owe him me life. The laugh on him, always chuckling at something. He'd lol at paint drying.
One of those infectious ones that gets everyone going.
During his Leaving he started going to laughing yoga at the local community centre, to ease the exam stress apparently.
Dragged me along one day. I told him, I says, sure I'm so chillaxed I'm horizontal. I need laughing yoga like I need a hole in the head. But I went along, to keep him sweet, communed with a bunch of strangers sitting in a circle pissing themselves. And believe it or not, I actually had a laugh.

Maz   That's a pretty unusual hobby for a Leaving Cert lad, isn't it?

Bricks   Absolute freak of nature.

Maz   Well, sounds like he's pretty enlightened.

Bricks   Ya, you could say that I suppose. Hey, is this what Tinder feels like?

Maz   What?

Bricks   You know, the saucy swiping app?

Maz   I am aware of it, yes.

Bricks   Is this what it feels like?

Maz   Tinder doesn't feel like anything apart from a cramp in your thumb, and death in your soul.

Bricks   So you're a fan then?

Maz   Dating isn't really my thing.

Bricks   I've never used it myself. Never have trouble getting ladies in real life.

Maz   So I hear.

Bricks   It kind of feels like we're tindering right now though, doesn't it.

Maz   You think confessing to me that you're an alcoholic as I get wasted and you sip Fanta 'feels like Tinder'?

Bricks   Wooooah! Hold your horses there, love; this is Club Orange. I wouldn't touch Fanta with a barge pole. Tastewise there's no comparison, it leaves Fanta in the gutter. And as for the ads on the telly. Fucking genius. Do remember yer man with the bushy orange eyebrows?

Maz   Vaguely . . .

Bricks   Absolute legend. Thaaank you for aaaaasking!

Maz   You don't actually think this is a date, do you?

Bricks   Thaaaaank you for asking.

Maz   Cos, it's one hundred percent absolutely not.

Bricks   Thaaaaank you for asking.

Maz   I'm not asking, I'm telling.

Bricks   D'ya want a sip? It's fucking delicious. Much easier on the liver than that Heineken pish.

Maz   I'm alright thanks.

Bricks   Seriously though, if you ever want to give it up, don't bother with all that twelve-step AA bullshit. It's a fucking racket. Have a sip of this stuff you'll never look back.

And I'm on the verge of winning her over with my
trusty drink of choice when I hear a familiar voice
behind me. I turn and it's Gav, Anto's closest
friend. Joined at the hip they were till the bitter,
drowned out end. I haven't seen this Gav chap in
months. I wasn't avoiding him, per se, but it was
me and him who took the brunt of Anto's death,
and I found it easier to keep my distance. I had this
weird resistance to seeing him, like when I looked
at him it was Anto staring back. And he's heading
towards me, and I'm not introducing him to Maz,
not if you paid me a fucking whack. I've just got
her back half on-side. She'd up and leave this pub,
no ifs or buts if she knew half the Anto shite.

'Gav, big man, how are ya?'

'Bricksy. Fuckin' hell. Good to see you man!
Jesus it's been a while.'

'Ya, haven't seen you in . . .'

'A year. Tomorrow.'

'Time flies wha.'

'Ya. It's madness. Listen, Bricks, I'm glad I ran into
ya.'

'Gav, I'm actually on a date would you believe it.
Kindle. Tinder. So I'm gonna have to love you and
leave ya.'

'Bricksy. Before you go I just wanted to say –'

'I'd love to chat t'ya, but can't keep the
missus waiting you know.'

'Course, man. Look I can't make the anniversary
mass tomorrow. I'm sorry, Bricksy.'

'No worries.'

'Tell your ma I say hi anyway. Fuck sake. A year. I miss him.'

Maz   And as this lad chats to him, the colour drains from Bricks' face, like he's morto uncomfortable, full on disgraced to be seen with me. And I'm thinking, alright I may not be the best fucking chat, but the last time I checked I'm not that unbearable either. But under my skin I've the fear maybe I am, and I take this as my cue to fuck off. Alright, this Bricks-through-windows lad might have won me over for a singular drink, but if he's worried, if he thinks I'm gonna plague him for even a micro second more. He's wrong. I down the last of my pint and head for the door.

Bricks   'See ya round, Gav.'

'Good luck at the mass, Bricksy. I'll be thinking of ya, tomorrow. It's fuckin' sad but remember: this too shall pass.'

And I have an overwhelming urge to punch him in the face, to knock out every one of his teeth and replace them with a mouthful of warm red blood.

I shouldn't have even spoke to him, the fucking cheek of him, to bring up the mass, when I'm trying to enjoy a fucking Club Orange in peace. And as I'm trying and failing to temper my temper I see Maz about to leave.

Bricks   Where are you off to?

Maz   I'm leaving.

Bricks   I thought we were having a drink?

Maz   I finished mine.

Bricks   I'll get you another.

Maz   I think I'll pass.

Bricks   I'll get ya a Club.

Maz   I don't want a fucking Club.

Bricks   I thought we were having a good time.

Maz   So did I. And then your friend arrived and you acted like I was fucking diseased. Couldn't get away from me quick enough. It's grand, I get it, the whole 'abortionist' chat is funny when it's banter on the Luas. But you don't want your mates knowing you hang around with someone who actually had one.

Bricks   Maz, it wasn't like that.

Maz   Was it not? Then why were you so desperate to get that guy as far away from me as humanly possible?

Bricks   Cos he's a cunt.

Maz   Really? Is he? Cos I'm pretty sure I heard him say 'good luck at the anniversary mass'. That's not a very cunty thing to do, since you insist on using that disgusting word.

Bricks   Maz, please. You have this all wrong.

Maz   No, *you* have this wrong. I gave you a chance. I don't have the headspace for this.

Bricks   Maz, I'm sorry. For being a dick on the Luas and sneaking up on ya at the march, and not introducing you to Gav. And I'm sorry that Eimear girl died, right? I swear it wasn't that I was embarrassed to be seen with you, it was nothing like that. I'm the fucking embarrassment. I'm sorry, I'm sorry, I'm sorry.

Maz   His brows furrowed like a field freshly ploughed, like if only I'd allow him the airtime he'd spew sorries till the Dublin cows come home. And as much as I'd give my right arm not to be alone today I feel like I've been fucking played. I dunno how I let it go this far, how I'm storming out of this bar feeling like a tipsy fool. But

something makes me hesitate, like maybe somehow
I've mistaken him and he's mistook me, and maybe
for once the answer is not to flee. Breeeeathe.

Bricks And I'm thinking this is not the kind of girl you
meet every day. She's fucking razor sharp, she's not
afraid to say what she thinks, she's also definitely
fucked in the head. I'd be lying if I said that wasn't
part of the allure and I'm so sure she's about to
ditch me for good, and I should let her off, I know I
should. But I'd sell my soul to have the foggiest
what's going on in those eyes. She has me inside
out, borderline hypnotized. And yes, I'll admit she's
an absolute ride, but it's not just her body I want,
it's her scrambled mind. Maz. This strange stranger.
And then next thing I do floors me, with how
fucking dangerous it is, out of the blue, I haven't a
clue what's come over me. But I commit.

Bricks *kisses* **Maz.**

* * *

Maz When I surface from a fairly gob-smacking kiss,
we're at the foot of the Ha'penny Bridge, I look
around and see things have taken a serious twist
for the worse. We've been encircled by a ten strong
hen party, penis balloons and L-plate signs, selfie
sticks, cheap t-shirts designed to depict the bride
lying face down with her knickers on display,
victims of the kind of weekend away I'd pay any
money *not* to go on.

'Oi love birds, get a fucking room.'

Bricks I turn sharpish, ready to deck whoever's slagging,
chins wagging, can two people not have an old
fashioned snog without being ridiculed, flogged in
public?

Maz Fuck off, please. All of you. There's nothing to see here.

And the pink clad hens in their cowgirl hats look at me like I'm bat shit crazy for telling them where to go. Like the kiss was some kind of a sick show they paid an arm and leg for, and now they're demanding an encore.

I said fuck off.

Bricks   Maz's tone rains on the parade, I'm not quite sure if she's humiliated or outraged.

But she's lost her cool, and I thought she was smart but she's a fuckin' fool, to start on a party of vodka-fuelled women in stilettos. And then she gets all up in the bride-to-be's face, like a woman possessed, aggressive, invading her personal space.

Maz   Oh and before you piss off tell me this. What's the fucking appeal in getting married in the Catholic church? Cos personally I think it's disgusting.

And I do. And bride-to-be here may not have the highest IQ, but she *knew*, I'm willing to bet she was perfectly aware of all the church's sins. She's like a blinkered horse, see the world in whatever shade you want, send out the invites in scrawly font, pack the relatives in like sardines in the pews, pretend like the thousands of people who were abused, have nothing remotely to do with you and your fairy-tale wedding.

Bricks   I can see the violence festering in the frontal lobe of Maz's brain, I've just clocked that she wouldn't have an ounce of shame in giving the bride a black eye as a wedding present, instead of what is it people give each other these days? Blenders?

The bride retaliates, she spits as she speaks.

Maz   'Ya so what's it to you if my wedding's in a Catholic church, ya fucking jealous dragon!'

Bricks   Up to now I've just been a surprised spectator but this is only gonna get worse if it goes any further. I snatch the bride's veil, shove it on my head and peg it.

Maz   'That's my fucking veil!'

He takes off and the party is after him, clucking and screaming, we're legging it over the bridge, through Temple Bar, he's dodging, weaving in and out of confused passers-by, the bride desperately trying and failing to keep up, I follow too. Who knew a lad like Bricks would ever have such a posse of women in his wake.

Bricks   And Maz is beaming, she's high on the chase. She's close behind me and her face has a look of a sprinter about to win gold, and as we leg it further from the party, this mad fiasco is getting old. I should probably fling the veil back like a bouquet, sail it through the air to one of the hens gagging to be next, but when I look behind they've disappeared. Couldn't hack the pace.

Maz   I think we've lost them.

Maz   We've finally shaken our pursuers and we're catching our breath. Bricks still has the veil on his head and like a coy bride he raises it real slow, and I think he might kiss me again. Then at least I can know whether it was a one-off phenomenon, a fluke in my gut, a rush of insanity. One more kiss, deep on the mouth, will bring me to my senses, straighten this out. But when he lifts his veil, his doily head-dress, I see his face is stony unimpressed.

Maz   You're a fucking state in that thing.

Bricks   I'm a state? Says yer one after attacking an innocent hen party? You're like some mad angry fox on a rampage.

Maz   You're the one who stole her veil.

Bricks   To distract from what a cunt you were being.

Maz   I was winding her up, bantering.

Bricks   No, you were being a full on cunt.

Maz   Don't use the C-word, it doesn't suit you. And neither does that.

Bricks *takes off the veil.*

Bricks   Does it not? So why are you looking at me like you're gagging to be kissed, smack bang in the middle of the altar?

Maz   Fuck you.

Maz *turns to go.*

Bricks   No, seriously. You might not love the church, most people don't, but abusing that bride like that for getting married? I get it. God's a myth, and priests are paedos. It's not her fault. Maybe she has a shit life and she feels like dressing up in a glorified communion dress for a day. Maybe she can't think of anything better to do than spend a couple of grand on a tacky party she'll be too drunk to remember. Maybe she genuinely wants to take her vows before Christ Jesus. It's her fucking life. See your outburst back there, frankly it was shameful.

Maz   What do you know about shame?!

Bricks   Plenty.

Maz   Oh what, you grew up on the north side and when you're walking home at night people cross the road cos they think you're gonna mug them. That's not shame, Bricks.

Bricks   Tallaght's on the southside, love. Get your facts straight. You don't have a fucking clue.

Maz   Do I not?

Bricks   No you don't have the slightest notion. You've plenty opinions, you've made that clear, but you don't –

Maz   I was abused OK?!

Bricks   Ah Christ.

Maz   Christ on a bike. Dark isn't it.

Bricks   Yes it is.

Maz   Sorry if I'm making you uncomfortable. Again.

Bricks   I'm not uncomfortable, I'm trying to . . .

Maz   Look. It's not . . . It was years ago. It's in the past, and it's fine now. I'm fine.

Bricks   You're obviously not fuckin' fine.

Maz   I wasn't humiliating the bride-to-be. I'm just sick of this country's selective memory, its straight up denial of every bad thing, every life ruined. Every day the church gets pardoned. Every day, men get pardoned. The girl who died yesterday, she'll be forgotten this time next week. People, Irish people, we have this brilliant, deluded ability to bury our heads in the sand, to forgive and forget.

Bricks   We're ostriches, aren't we. It's no one's fault, it's just . . .

Maz   What do you mean it's no one's fault ?

Bricks   I'm not saying that. I just mean it's a coping mechanism, pretending shit never happened.

Maz   I know. And I'm guilty of it too. Jesus. I should still be out there protesting with the women who can actually hold their nerve. I'm a fucking hypocrite.

Bricks   You're not.

Maz   That girl could have been me.

Silence.

And it's rising up in me like thick hot bile, the
thoughts I thought too wrong, too vile to attach
words to are coming up spewing out of me with a
freedom I haven't known, like my mouth's been
sewn up till now and he's ripped it open with some
unseen power, and the words taste bitter strange,
sweet and sour, like a Chinese takeaway you think's
an inspired plan, until five minutes in you can
barely stand how sick you feel.

Bricks   I'm listening. (*Silence.*) Look at me. You're alright.

Maz   I can't believe I'm saying this out loud. I turned
seventeen the day I realized I was pregnant. Nicked three
tests from the chemist and they were all positive. So I told
my mam. I don't know what I expected, maybe that she'd
leave him. Mick. Her boyfriend. That she'd leave him and
help me? She spat on me when I told her. I remember so
clearly looking down at her saliva on my new runners.

She said it was my fault. That I was asking for it. That I
wanted it. And maybe I did, you know in some twisted way.
I liked him. In the beginning. The attention. The feeling
that some one wanted me. The power I suppose. I didn't
get on with my mam, I always pissed her off, or
disappointed her. And with him I felt like finally I mattered,
that I was somebody.

But then it started happening more, like a lot but it all just
spiralled and . . . by the end I was afraid to come home. I felt
so trapped. And then I got pregnant, then I really knew
what trapped felt like.

Bricks   Fucking hell.

Maz   And then my mam tried to stop me going to England.
And I fought her and fought her, and all this time I had this
thing growing in me. That reminded me of him. Every
second. I couldn't sleep, I couldn't eat. A neighbour, this
woman who used to babysit me, she gave me money and
helped me get to England. I saw her today, at the demo. She

was pregnant. She always wanted a kid of her own. And it just made me think about my mam and how I haven't spoken to her in three years.

Bricks   Do you miss her?

Maz   She fucking spat on me. (*Silence.*) I don't know. She tried to contact me a few times. And she sends me stuff on my birthday. As if a fifty euro note and socks from Penneys' is gonna air brush the past.

Bricks   She'll die of some horrible incurable disease.

Maz   What?

Bricks   Your mam. As karma. She'll pop her clogs any day now.

Maz   Is that meant to make me feel better?

Bricks   Or else she'll cop on to herself and make it up to you and live a long and healthy life. If that's what you'd prefer?

Maz   I'm not sure. I think I need to flip a coin.

Bricks   Heads she lives, tails she dies.

Maz   Oh God.

Bricks   I know. This is a very flippant game wha'? Tell me if I'm being insensitive.

Maz   Nah, it's fine.

Bricks *flips a coin.*

Bricks   And the verdict is . . .

Maz   Don't tell me.

Bricks   Ah don't lie, you're dying to know. *Dying.*

Maz   Go on so.

Bricks   Tails! Ding dong the witch is dead.

Maz *starts laughing, and then crying.*

Maz   I do miss her. Sometimes.

Bricks   Course you do, love. I was only messing with ya. Don't be crying, love. Here, would it help if I put this back on?

Bricks *puts the veil on, and takes her hands.*

You're great, you know that. You are brilliant and you're brave.

Bricks *raises the veil.*

And you may kiss the –

Maz   Don't say the B-word.

Bricks   You may kiss the Bricks.

* * *

Maz   And he's ditched the veil, and we're on Dame Street now, heading nowhere in particular, just wandering aimless. An unlikely, shifting shameless pair.

Maz   Would you rather have vaginas for eyebrows, or a penis for a nose?

Bricks   Are you serious? We used to play this game in third class.

Maz   Answer the questions.

Bricks   I feel sick, so I do, thinking of period blood trickling down into my eyes.

Maz   C'mon, vag brows or a willy nose?

Bricks   No comment.

Maz   Go with your gut.

Bricks   Well, I'd be to embarrassed to have me willy standing to attention in the middle of my face every two seconds, wouldn't I?

Maz   Vaginas for eyebrows. I respect your decision. I'll sort you out with a pair of mooncups and you'll be laughing.

Bricks   What are mooncups?

Maz   Google it. Question two. If you could have one super power, what would it be?

Bricks   One super power, that's a tough one, that is. I have a top three.

Maz   You only get one.

Bricks   Ya stingy bitch, I want three.

Maz   OK, well let me hear them and I'll decide.

Bricks   One: I'd like to be able to walk through glass doors. Imagine the looks on people's faces when you step through a sliding door like fucking Casper the friendly ghost. Two: I'd like to be able to time travel. I'd go back to Saipan and convince Roy Keane to take his head out of his arse, eat his prawn sandwiches and do his bit for his country. The prick.

Maz   Right . . .

Bricks   Three: I'd like to have the power to communicate with wasps.

Maz   With wasps?

Bricks   They're dicks, aren't they. I'd get in amongst them and I'd be like 'Lads, why all this anger? This terrorism. Take a leaf outta the bees' book and chill the fuck out'. I'd start a wasp revolution. Me and Yas watched *The Incredibles* the other day. A massive pile of shite so it was. Mr Strong and Mrs Elastic. Please. Get Mr Wasp Whisperer on the go.

Maz   You should pitch that to Pixar. They would eat that shit up.

Bricks   You think ?

Maz   Eh no. OK. Last question. If you could bring one person back to life who would you choose?

Bricks   Your mam. I feel bad for killing her off.

Maz   You're hysterical. I'm serious you have to answer this one.

Bricks   My brother Anto.

Maz   Wait, the brother who does laughing yoga?

Bricks   Used to. He died. A year ago tomorrow.

Maz   Oh God, I didn't know.

Bricks   I know you didn't.

Maz   I'm so sorry, Bricks.

Bricks   It's not your fault. Here. I'm not being harsh right, I just think it's stupid the way people trip over themselves apologising when they find out someone's dead. 'I'm sorry', 'sorry for your loss', 'sorry for your troubles'. It's like no you're fucking not, you're just shaking my sweaty hand in a funeral home that smells like feet and rotten flowers and you can't think of anything to say. It's me who's fucking sorry.

Maz   You're right. It's pathetic. Sorry.

Bricks   I'll have to start a fucking sorry jar with you around. I'll be minted.

Maz   How did he die?

Bricks   Hardly matters now, does it. Look, I'm not trying to shut you down. But it's his anniversary mass tomorrow and there'll be tears enough then. Cry me a fucking river.

Maz   I just presumed, the way you were talking about him, that he was still. . .

Bricks   Ya, in my head he is. Living, breathing, sleeping, pissing, pissing me off. I can hear him laughing at me, snoring like a fucking troll, slurping beans. He was mad for beans, not Heinz. Like any normal person. But HP. Like he was some kind of fuckin' Brit trapped in a Irishman's body. Yas loves them too. He started her on them. He taught her how to smack her plastic spoon off her high chair and chant HP HP HP. She doesn't remember him well. She was only three when it happened, but she still chants that when she wants beans. HP HP HP. She think it's hilarious.

Maz   Yas sounds like a joker.

Bricks   She's hysterical.

Bricks *smiles sadly and checks his phone.*

Bricks   The anniversary mass is in a Catholic church, d'ya reckon I should boycott it?

Maz   I think this is an exceptional circumstance.

Bricks   I was meant to have Yas tomorrow. There's something about little people. They're so pure, so hopeful that they make the darkest shit bearable. But now that Lara is withholding her from me, I'm tempted to pull a sickie.

Maz   I'm sure she'll get in touch eventually.

Bricks   Ya, the next time she needs a babysitter so she can go out and get new talons glued to her fingers. What d'ya ma call it? Shellac.

Maz   All the better for scratching your eyes out with.

Bricks   And I probably deserve it, to be honest. Look, if she wants to spend half the children's allowance on plastic nails, I'll make peace with it. I make peace with everything, eventually. You have to.

Maz   Really? Do you feel at peace with your brother, with Anto . . .

Bricks   Being dead? You can say it. The D-word. He didn't slip away, or pass over, he's stone dead.

Maz   Right. Are you OK with Anto being dead?

Bricks   I'm fuckin' light years away from forgiveness, if
that's what you mean. But you have to be open to it don't
you, otherwise it eats you from the inside. Like some kind of
aggressive tapeworm. Ya know what I mean, don't you, Maz.
You know where I'm coming from.

Maz   Ya, I do.

* * *

Bricks   We've wandered up past the Grafton Street
buskers, the chain-smoking flower hustlers, the too
many mobile phone shops, the emos with the hair
that flops in their moody black eyes, the man
making a sand dog the size of a beached whale
outside BT's, some Red Bull promoters giving out
the poison for free, (*To the promoter*) not a fucking
chance love. Wings my hole. That stuff gives ya
erectile dysfunction!

I see Butlers on the horizon, and I feel a gulf
forming in me tummy, I need a sugar hit, that
fuzzy feeling you get when a chocolate worth a
fiver melts in your mouth. Mine's salivating already
like the fucking sand Labrador at the thought.

Bricks   I'd murder a fancy chocolate, so I would.

Maz   I'll get ya one so.

Bricks   You serious?

Maz   Ya, I'm feeling generous. Any requests?

Bricks   Anything as long as it's not an alcoholic truffle. I'll
be pissed in the gutter after one bite.

Maz   I eye roll him and take note. Could a single boozy
chocolate sink his AA boat? I won't tempt fate, not
at this late hour in this bitter sweet day. Butlers is
rammed, jammed with people deliberating over

their complimentary chocolate like their lives are at
stake, like the choice they make, be it salted
caramel or Turkish delight, is red pill blue pill
death or life.

I dabbled in kleptomania back in the day, I
remember when aged six it dawned on me that you
didn't actually have to pay. It was optional, by
donation you could say. It started with the jelly
snakes, I was a sucker for the sweet, squidgy
E-numbered taste, that giddy high, in my tiny
mind, as I pocketed ten, sauntered out, thinking
'it'll be fried eggs the next time'.

But it's been a while and I'd forgotten that thrill,
skulking, gulping down the terror, going in for the
kill. It's a physical reflex before I even make up my
mind, my body's rebelling, refusing to wait in this
obnoxious chocolate line. Out of the corner of my
eye as I spot a shiny, fuck off box. I aim and fire,
and it drops into my safe hands, flips and lands
with a satisfying rattle. Then I turn on my heels
and battle my way out. When I find Bricks he's
staring in awe. Lot's wife turned to stone. Like one
rebellious stunt and his mind is blown.

Bricks   You are mad to get arrested. You're gagging for it.
Beating up grannies, nicking chocolates.

Maz   You gonna open them or what?

Bricks   I want to tell her right now I'd rather undress her
than the stolen sweets, this kleptomaniac woman
makes my heart soar and beat quicker than it has in
a long while. I'm ahead of myself by a country mile,
I know, so I keep schtum. Curb my enthusiasm and
bite my tongue.

Maz   I can't deal with this dawdling business, so I rip the
lid off, choose one and throw one full force at his
head. It's round, white chocolate and hits him

square between the eyes. The size and look of a golf ball, it makes a dull thud against his skull, then falls to the grass. He drops to his knees like an absolute fool and retrieves it yelping.

Bricks   Ten second rule!

Maz   We're in Stephen's Green now skirting round the pond. It feels like someone wove a wand and I'm almost . . . light. Less heavy. Giddy, borderline drunk. I've blocked out the day that's in it. I'm silly as a skunk my mother would have said. Maybe the spiked truffles have gone to my head. I toss one to the ducks. Bread is so 2016.

Bricks   And a passing granny opens her toothless gob, half joking. I take aim and expertly lob in a dark chocolate surprise and she smiles and closes her wrinkly eyes in pleasure. I feel like we're feeding the masses. Every person who passes gets one aimed and fired. It's like the fishes and the loaves. The kids are flocking in droves. Until every last one of the fancy chocolates has been devoured.

Maz   And we're at the far side of the park, and I hear cries floating through the Dublin sky, and it hits me like a bus, that this afternoon was a lie. That this pathetic Bricks attachment, my hen party harassment, this chocolate flinging, it was all just winning me an escape from the march. Which is coming to an end, which is congregating just up the road and around the bend. And the sound of the masses sends guilt through me like shock waves. And Bricks is looking at me but I don't know what to say. My mouth is dry, laced with sugary regret and Turkish delight.

Bricks   Right. Let's get back on that fucking march. As long as you swear not to get arrested.

Maz   And it's like he can see the addled contents of my
mind, all buzzing and whirring like the inside of a
grandfather clock. And I'm not sure how wise this
plan is but relief floods through me. I'm high on
the belief that I can salvage this. As we exit the
park we join the sprawling march, headed towards
Merrion Square. The pair of us slip into it like
we've been there since the heated get go. And I'm
a drop in an angry ocean, no one will ever know
that I was dossing off with him. That I didn't have
it in me to march with the thousands of foot
soldiers, that I'm a traitor of the highest order.

Bricks *takes* **Maz***'s hand.*

Bricks   In case I lose you. And get killed in a stampede of
abortionists. Also if I'm holding your hand it doesn't count
as stalking.

Maz   And he slips his hand into mine, like it's an
extension of his, I think of retracting it, telling him
the PDA is out of line. That whatever about a kiss,
this is too far. This 'raise the bar and pretend we're
a couple', it makes me want to double over in fear
of what's to come. I want to tell him that
everything's easier when I'm on my own. That
there's a reason I don't let anyone even remotely
close to home. But I don't. Because for the first
time in God knows how long, I feel like I belong to
someone.

Bricks   'Never again!' they cry. It's like being at a gig, only
more hair-raising. And they're all chanting and
rhyming all clever phrasing. 'Not the church, not
the state, women must decide their fate'!

Maz   'Not in our name, and not on our watch,' another
woman sacrificed another life bludgeoned,
botched. History repeating, women dying while
men in power go on living sleeping, breathing,

cheating us out of lives. Stealing the breath out of lungs, fucking us blue, until they've 3, 2, 1 come, unpicked, unravelled, undone us. Gone and strung us up and sauntered out.

Bricks   The pain in this crowd is vivid, like it nearly has a colour, like if it was any fuller with raw emotion it'd explode. Like it's a loaded paintball gun, like if anyone pulled the trigger the place would be drenched in incriminated red.

Maz   And no matter what sob story we tell, we remain mere numbers, statistics. Tipp-exed over 'cases', bodies, vessels, faceless beings. The infamous X case, Ms Y asylum seeker raped. And for those of us named and shamed Eimear Colgan the latest victim, Joanne Hayes and her Kerry twins, Anne Lovett and her graveyard sins, Savita Halappanavar, it doesn't change a thing. It doesn't alter the state we're in.

Bricks   And she'll never know, but I'm less of a stranger than she thinks. I've lived on the crumbling edges of sadness too. I lost someone who this country failed. And his story might pale and fade in comparison to this Eimear girl they're marching for but as Maz grips me tighter, curls her fingers round mine, I squeeze her small hand back to say 'you're gonna be fine'. Cos I have no words to put on any of this. But I want her to know, that despite the shit she's been through, the shit that has her black and blue with bruises, she's not on her own.

Maz   There's a blanket of exhaustion over our once wild fire cries, like each one of us is bearing a weight the size of this very nation on our shoulders. And as the last speech ends, and the crowd dissipates, I wonder vaguely if this is some kind of fake news story. Maybe it's an elaborate hoax. I'm waiting for someone to whisper in my ear that really she's alive, of course women aren't dying because the state refuses to save our lives. I think I'll be sick, like someone's gripping my insides in an iron fist. This cannot be it. I want someone to shake me from this twisted dream. One foot in front of the other, I'm weak at the knees. It's all over and what? Our outrage will be buried with her young body? And as we walk away there's a woman on a kerb quietly sobbing.

Bricks   And she's leading me God knows where, she's still wearing my hand on hers like it's a life-line. And this is the kind of thing that happens in films. You meet someone and they bring you to your knees. You blink, you fucking sneeze and you're bound up with them, wound up with them, you're protesting with them, you're following them unquestioning.

Maz   I'm numb with it this acute defeat, and I can't think of anything except I need to be beside the sea. I want to walk into the ocean, but that's impractical. My second best notion is to head for the Liffey. To the Rosie Hackett, my favourite bridge.

A woman of hope and vision and organisation, of tooth and nail, endless determination. Everything I'll never be. And if I can just dangle my feet off Rosie's section of the river. The pain in me might drift downstream. The snaking grey Liffey might wash me clean.

Maz *and* **Bricks** *are at the Rosie Hackett Bridge.* **Maz** *hops up onto the railings.*

Bricks   Get down ya mad bitch.

Maz   I love this bridge.

Bricks   That's great, now get the fuck down, you're giving me the heebie-jeebies.

Maz   Relax. I'm just checking out the rival bridges. They're all shit in comparison.

Bricks   Hardly.

Maz   They are. The Rosie Hackett is the queen of all bridges.

Bricks   The Dozie Hackface is not the queen of all bridges, you mad royalist.

Maz   Fine, the *goddess* of all bridges.

Bricks   She is in her hole. This bridge is bland as fuck.

Maz   Oi, have a bit of respect.

Bricks   Why should I?

Maz   Eh, because she was a shit hot trade unionist and a republican and one of the most influential working class women this country has every seen. That's why.

Bricks   Working class? That's sexy.

Maz   I didn't say it was sexy.

Bricks   No I did.

Maz   Well it's not.

Bricks   Ah, it is a bit though. To the likes of you.

Maz   What's that supposed to mean?

Bricks   You love a hard-nosed Dub as much as the next mot. Ah, come on admit it, there's a certain appeal.

Maz   You're full of shit.

Bricks   Don't lie, the accent, the attitude. Us Tallafornia lads are notoriously irresistible.

Maz   You think I fetishise you cos you grew up on a dodgy estate and wear Nike Air Max?

Bricks   Why else would you fancy me?

Maz   What makes you think I fancy you?

Bricks   I may not have done the Leaving, but I'm smarter than you think.

Maz   Fuck off.

Bricks *winks.*

Bricks   I wish I had a padlock on me. I can see it now. The pair of us. Maz and Bricks. Padlocked to the Rosie Hackett till death do us part.

Maz   I hate those locks.

Bricks   Romance is dead, is it?

Maz   Ya, I killed it. So tomorrow is your brother's mass.

Bricks   Don't fuckin remind me.

Maz   You gonna go?

Bricks   Fuck knows.

Maz   Maybe you should toss a coin. I hear it's a very scientific way of making serious life decisions.

Bricks   Go on so. You decide.

Maz   Gimme your euro.

Bricks *gives her his euro from earlier.*

Bricks   Thief.

Maz   Heads you go, tails I padlock you to the Rosie Hackett for life. Alone.

Maz *flips the coin.*

Maz   Heads.

Bricks   Suppose I better get home and iron my non-existent suit. I've been dreading tomorrow since he died. D'ya know why? I gave him an ultimatum to be back in a year, and if he wasn't then I'd get on with it without him.

No sign of him so far. Still a few hours to go. He might show up yet.

Maz   I'll keep my eyes peeled.

Bricks   If you see a mad bastard wandering around eating HP cold outta the tin let me know. You'd have liked him. You'd have fancied him. He was a better version of me.

Maz   Impossible.

Bricks   Fuck off. Nah. I should probably go. It's about time I got my shit together. This year I didn't really cope. I stopped drinking alright but that was mostly because I knew I'd come a cropper too if I didn't. But me head was still a fucking jungle. Sometimes even now I think I should just go back on it, fuck it. Raid the offies and drink myself to oblivion.

Maz   I know that feeling.

Bricks   I'm so fucking lucky I've Yas. It's mind blowing, how this little creature can just come into your life and make you a better person. She's the reason I wake up every morning. She's the reason I can't hate Anto forever, for leaving me.

Maz   It must be nice to have something in your life that matters so much.

Bricks   What about you?

Maz   What about me?

Bricks   What's your reason for getting out of bed in the morning?

Maz *shrugs*.

Maz   I'm not sure I have one.

Bricks   That's not true.

Maz   I dunno. I guess I just want to be normal. I don't know how that feels, but it's all I want.

Bricks   I don't think anyone knows how normal feels.

Maz   I'm just sick of being angry. At my mam, at him. At this country. Because they all fucked me over and somehow made me feel like I deserved it. On some level I still feel like I do. I'm trying to forget it all, I really am. But no matter how much I drink, or how much numbing medication I take. I can't. I get it, anger is toxic, and unattractive and destructive. Being so full of rage that you can't sleep at night doesn't change a thing. I don't know. I just don't want anger to be my life.

Bricks   Anger's not all bad. Like if you channel it. That's what brought you on the march, isn't it?

Maz   We won't dwell on the fact that I skived off most of it.

Bricks   You travelled from the back arse of nowhere for today, didn't you. That's admirable.

Maz   Is it? I don't know what I thought would happen. That if enough people showed up she would come back to life? Watching everyone just go their separate ways at the end . . . it's really fucking sad.

Bricks   I was thinking, back there, about Yas. That all that shit is ahead of her. When she grows up. Like how I'd feel . . . if what happened to you happened to her. Makes me sick.

Maz   It's easy to think like that now, while she's a perfect, innocent four-year-old.

Bricks   Her age has nothing to do with it.

Maz   I'm just saying, little girls are easy to love, then they get older, they get lippy, they sleep around, they piss their daddies off. And suddenly they're not so cute any more. And when really bad shit happens to them, it's their fault. They deserved it. And they'll be punished for it.

Bricks   I will never ever let that happen to Yas. I won't. She will always be my little girl. I'd die to protect her. I'd kill to protect her.

Maz   She doesn't need your protection. She doesn't need a fucking macho bodyguard.

Bricks   I'm her da!

Maz   What she needs is respect.

Bricks   Of course I fucking respect her. She hasn't even started school and she's smarter than me already.

Maz   Do you respect women in general?

Bricks   Who exactly is 'women in general'?

Maz   Well, do you respect Lara?

Bricks   Honestly? No I don't. If she wants my respect she'll have to earn it.

Maz   She's the mother of your child.

Bricks   She's a fucking demon.

Maz   Is she though? You say that but have you ever actually tried to see things from her perspective? Even once? Cos I'm willing to bet the world would look very fucking different from where she's standing.

Bricks   Get down off your moral high horse, will ya? Ya fine, we all have our own versions of events. No, I don't see the world from Lara's twisted point of view. That doesn't make me a bad father, or a bad person. That's fucking life. If you bit the bullet, called up your mam, and asked her about the last five years I bet you two would have different stories.

Maz   My mam has nothing to do with this!

Bricks   Does she not?

Silence.

Maz   Fuck it. I'm not busy tomorrow.

Bricks   I am according to your coin toss.

Maz   If you wanted I could . . . come with you. To the church.

Bricks   Mazzie.

Maz   Don't call me that. Only my mam called me Mazzie. I hate it. (*Silence.*) The church thing was a stupid idea.

Bricks   It's just with Yas and Lara and all. As I said, it's complicated.

Maz   Of course it is.

Bricks   And today was beautiful. Really fucking sad, you know, with the march and all, but meeting you was beautiful. And I, I just think we shouldn't ruin it.

Maz   How would we ruin it?

Bricks   Humans have a talent for ruining things. At least this human does. As you know.

Maz   Oh come on, Bricks, give yourself some credit.

Bricks   I'm telling you, Maz. You don't wanna get involved with me. Everything I touch turns to shite. Trust me.

Maz   I didn't say anything about getting involved with you.

Bricks   Good.

Maz   So this is it? After today, your ideal scenario would be to never see me again.

Silence.

You're a dick.

Bricks   Ya, you're fucking right. I am a dick. And I'm telling you for your own good to stay away from me.

Maz   Kiss me.

Bricks   Maz . . .

Maz   Please. I want you to kiss me.

Maz *leans in to kiss* **Bricks**. **Bricks** *turns away.*

Bricks   You have a brilliant mind, you know. And a brilliant soul. Why don't you believe that? This drives me mad, you know that. Why can't the best fucking people look in the mirror and see what they're worth?

Maz   I'm obviously not that brilliant if you don't want to see me again.

Bricks   It's not like that.

Maz   I don't know what today was. All I know is that it doesn't feel like it was an accident.

Bricks   Ya, I know. And that's why I can't . . .

Maz   If you don't want to see me again just say it.

Bricks   I don't want to see you again.

Maz   It's as if a switch has flicked and he's had his bit of fun. I'm just another one of his long line of fucking mots. I've taken my precious time but I'm finally joining the dots and I get it. I was wrong if I thought he remotely gave a shit.

Bricks   I know what I said is backward and cruel, and I know I've fucked it, I'm a fool for her and I'm pushing shoving arms lengthing her away, but it's not fair of her to take what I say and twist it completely, I won't have that, I'm tired of people repeatedly insisting on painting me by fucking numbers as something I am not. And it isn't that I don't want to see her, it's just that already lines are getting blurred and crossed. We need to just pause. I want to tell her I can't handle how I feel, that today with her was too raw, too real.

Maz   And everything is swimming out of focus, and I don't know if he has noticed but his wish is

granted. He will never see me again. And it's not
because he's made it plain, he's made it Waterford
crystal clear he's no interest in me. It's bigger than
him. It's deeper, it's a hurt in the bones of me. It's a
thousand tiny straws that crippled the camel's back
and I'm my mother's china tea cups, cracked for
the longest time, and now I'm smashed into too
many pieces to ever superglue. There's too much
hurt to ever undo and my breaths are catching in
my lungs, they are sharp and few and I should tell
him that it's me not him, that of the thousand
things wrong in my life he isn't one, that he can
head on home, to his precious daughter. And
forget me.

Cos I'm better off on my own, I came to Dublin
today, alone, and that's how I'll leave.

Bricks   I don't want to see you again.

And I don't decide on those words they just sort of
slip from my lips and in the same moment she slips
from the bridge. I grab her, almost I have her by
the hips but they're narrower than they look and
in micro seconds she's gone from my grip. And
nothing makes any fucking sense. Like every ounce
of me has been used up, every grain of
determination spent on losing every good thing
that I've loved. It's my fault. I pushed her, I shoved
her off the fucking Rosie Hackett Bridge. Am I
gonna watch another one sink like a stone? Hit the
water like she's going home? Like they all belong in
the bottom of a river? Like all the cracks in their
broken lives don't let in even a sliver of light?
Fucking Christ, when you died was it for this? To
save us from the sins that would drown us? From a
world, a country that beats and batters and hounds
us till we have stones in our pockets and stones in

> our minds. And I can't go through this again. Not a second time.

Maz *slides off the bridge and into the water below.*

* * *

Maz *is in hospital after the Liffey incident.* **Bricks** *comes to visit with his daughter* **Yas**.

Bricks   'Ssssh, pet, she's asleep.'

'Daddy, why is the lady asleep?'

'Cos she's absolutely wrecked, so she is.'

'Why is she wrecked, Daddy?'

'She had a mad busy day yesterday. Walked for miles and went swimming in the Liffey.'

'Can I go swimming in the Liffey?'

'You can not. You're banned from rivers for life.'

'Why?'

'Cos you are.'

'Even with arm bands?'

'Even with arm bands.'

'Poor sick lady. Elsa will help her feel better.'

Elsa's plastic hand starts stroking Maz's face, her white bluish cheeks, in the bruised place where a tube is snaking into her nose. *Frozen* girl, knows how to cure even the most broken patients. Elsa herself is looking pretty wrecked. She's greying with the dirt, flecked with stains of God knows what. She might give you fleas she's that unwashed. But Yas loves her so unconditionally, so softly, that Elsa's fucking magic.

'She likes it. The lady likes when Elsa strokes her!'

'You sure about that?'

'What's the lady's name?'

'Her name is Maz.'

'That sounds like my name. I'm called Yas and she's called Maz! Daddy, is the lady your friend?'

'Yes, sweetheart. She is my friend.'

'Can she be my friend too?'

There's something breath-catchingly beautiful about Maz, Yas and Elsa face to face, three bright and brilliant women in this Godforsaken hospital place. And I'm shattered in my heart and my mind. I'm exhausted, shrouded in a weird fog the kind that protects you at the worst of times.

But I have Yas. Lara having relented, when presented with the facts about last night and my plunge into the Liffey, if she was iffy about me spending time with my own kid, I suppose she took what I did as a sign I put someone else first. For once in my life. And this shit with Maz was a high price to pay to get Yas back on this bleak anniversary day and I'm still in shock. It's safe to say I'm drowning out yesterday. I'm essentially pretending I'm not scarred from it all. That I didn't die a bit inside as I took that plunge, the fall in after Maz. A year to the day since Anto left us, called it quits, a beautiful lippy stranger flings herself off a bridge. You couldn't fuckin' make it up.

Maz *opens her eyes.*

'Look Da, Elsa woke her up!'

'Are you OK now, lady? Are you very tired after swimming? You should wear arm bands the next

time. You can borrow mine if you want. I have
Frozen arm bands.'

'My uncle Anto went swimming like you. He never
woke up. I wish he had my *Frozen* arm bands. It's
good you're awake. Elsa woke you up. I'm going to
light a candle for Anto with granny now. She
doesn't let me touch the fire though cos fire is
dangerous. Once Elsa's hair touched a candle but
she didn't go on fire. Phew.'

'Ssshhh babe. You'll wear her out with your mad
chat.'

And a nurse whisks Yas out of the room. And now
we are alone I want to make it known to Maz, that
while she's drugged up in her hospital daze, I'm
dealing with a fair amount of choking rage. That
what she did is so far from OK. That those of us
living we don't wallow in it. Instead we wash it
back, swallow it down with whatever dregs of a can
we get our desperate hands on. And I'm full of
deepest fear of the future, of the heartbreak
lurking around the bend. How many more fake
prayers am I gonna have to send up to a bullshit
God not to lose any more gems.

Maz I'm sorry.

Bricks Don't apologise.

Maz   No, I'm sorry.

Bricks I'll have to get the sorry jar out again.

Maz I didn't want you to . . . You weren't meant to come
after me.

Bricks Well, what did you expect? Look. It's fine. It's water
under the bridge.

Maz You have Yas . . .

Bricks   Ya. Lara changed her mind.

Maz   I'm glad.

Bricks   She knows, about everything. We're off to mass now.

Maz   Bricks, are you OK?

Bricks   I'm grand, sure. A year and a day off the drink. Hanging out with Maz and Yas. No complaints. Thank you for asking.

Maz   It wasn't cos of you, Bricks.

Bricks   You don't have to explain. I'm gonna go and get Yas.

Bricks *looks like he might cry. He takes* **Maz***'s hand.*

Bricks   I'll see ya.

Bricks *leaves.*

Maz   And they're gone, the pair of them, like a gust of fictitious wind, and I'm left alone with the silence and the state I'm in, the sedation like a thin layer of stale sleep over me.

They leave me a clump of strange brazen yellow dandelions, tied together with a blue elastic band. Hand-picked and presented by the tiny dainty Yas. A brilliant, bouncy human, the spit of her dad.

The nerve of me, I think, as what Yas said slips through my skin, goes deeper in my bones. I should have could have known, the reason one year on Anto's not alive, eating HP beans with his niece, cruising round town with Bricks, disturbing the peace. And although Anto's nothing to me but the ghost brother of Bricks, a name bandied around, hints fed to me in broken bits, I feel I know him now. Like I've pieced him together, traced him to the very end of his tether.

And a part of Bricks died, when Anto called it quits, broke his soul in a way that can never be fixed and what have I done only twisted the knife in his year deep wounds.

As my shame fills the hospital room, it dawns on me there's only one thing I can do, and it'll be in Anto's name too.

I'll swallow this pain and go on living, I'll cling to this unwanted chance I've been given.

'I want to use the phone.'

A nurse helps me down a sterile corridor, I place one foot in front of the purple, blue other. Disinfectant and silence and the squeak of rubber.

Step, step, step. I pick up the phone. And I don't know why or what the tumble out of my dry mouth words will be. And it takes me three attempts to dial the number even though I know it backward off by hammering heart. I've practiced the words for three years, I'm cold sweating, sick with fear of no answer, of rejection again, of what I will or won't hear if I let it ring.

Maz *picks up the phone to call her mum.*

'Hi, Mam? . . . It's Mazzie . . .'